MW01254595

MORTAL
ARGUMENTS

MORTAL
ARGUMENTS

๛ SUE SINCLAIR

Brick Books

National Library of Canada Cataloguing in Publication

Sinclair, Sue, 1972-
        Mortal arguments / Sue Sinclair.

Poems.
ISBN 1-894078-29-2

        I. Title.

PS8587.I55278M67 2003   C811'.6   C2003-903694-4

Copyright© Sue Sinclair, 2003
Second Printing – September 2007

We acknowledge the support of the Canada Council for the Arts, the Government of Canada through the Book Publishing Industry Development Program (BPIDP), and the Ontario Arts Council for their support of our publishing program.

   Canada Council   Conseil des Arts
          for the Arts   du Canada

The painting on the cover is by Sophie Thériault, *Nature morte* (detail) 2003, oil on canvas, 30 in. by 40 in.

This book is set in Sabon.

Design and layout by Alan Siu.
Printed and bound by Sunville Printco Inc.

Brick Books
431 Boler Road, Box 20081
London, Ontario N6K 4G6

www.brickbooks.ca

CONTENTS

Patience

Abundance

Birthday

Light dumped on our heads,
we become heaven's compost. Our thoughts,
like insects, chew through eternity's lost
causes, hours and days, time's least
digestible fibres. We take in what heaven can't
or won't put up with: living and dying,
the incomplete virtues of strength and weakness. It's not true
there is no fear in heaven: the gods keep
watch over us, are afraid of the losses
we hold, afraid to die. They don't trust
their own endlessness. You are the natural outcome
of immortality's inability to conceive.
The one thing it can't bear, which is why it needs you.

Prime

Dragonflies hover in tandem, glued
together at the ends
like the trees reflected in the pond, everything
in pairs,
    multiple,
        lily pads
rucked up against
each other, some lifted
from the water
like heroes carried home
on shoulders: frogs
ping like rubber bands,

the buzz, the glitter, flashbulbs
popping, so this
is where media was born,

its meaning asway
in the lushness of place,
full of ears, alert:

the world sits up, attentive,
listens to the story of itself from
beginning to end,

applauds wildly.

Vacation

The ocean roams
like a stray dog, whose name

no one knows, who's been
coming around so long

we don't bother guessing.
We lean back into the tired joints

of beach chairs and imagine our lives
as white lies. Waves

roll on the sand, and it's again
the dog, who won't tell

where his bone is buried. We don't care.
Two weeks go by and only when

we're leaving, watching from the train,
do we know what we came for: to look back

at the shining sand, the ocean
stretched out under the sky. The shore,

as we go, lies open,
broken locket, weak hinge.

Witness I

Light says we should redistribute
the wealth, touches every surface. Its argument
is your own mortality: *is* becomes *ought*.

Children in the glassed-in pool
learn to swim, snapping their legs together
like mousetraps. Under your very nose, a thing becomes itself
by changing into another. The struggle
illuminates your own purposes:
never more than today

have you wanted to save the world, which means
moving as slowly as you can, as if life were a hive of bees
you dare not disturb. The greater good
is all around, buzzes as you look down at the pool,
the water aquamarine.

Springtime

The maples woo the car, its hood covered in pollen.

Nature attempts the impossible yet again, the only way it knows
of coping with a dead end.

Longing wants to fuse with use.

What's a white Volvo to do? Without genetics, without family or
anyone to follow it home.

Pollen under the windshield wipers, in all the intimate corners.

It's pure engine, can't think except in the past tense of fossil
fuels.

Who's to say nature can't turn it into something more? There's no
better time or place.

If there's any more luck in the world, let it find its way here.

Paddling

The shine, the square of light on every leaf,
lilies, more leaves, the V of the canoe in the water: gateway
to nowhere, the beginning of imagining you aren't.

Fear of profusion: where things are few, they seem
necessary. The trees and their thousand leaves massed
on the verge of disappearance.

Light clamps onto us, we'll have to skin ourselves
to be rid of it. Paddles dip in the water, dip and pretend
they don't know what goes on, don't see the world vanishing.

In the mind's mud, nothingness spawns. Where time becomes less
pressing, we feel its depth. The world is burnished: trees, bark, skin
going up in flame. The gods are not what you hoped they would be.

The sun, taking us all down with it.
Heedless, the ten thousand things.

Backyard

Buddleia, hydra-headed, loses track
of the array of itself. Fear begins in such instants:
the flowering bush calls out, mired in blossoms,
emptiness at the root.

Everywhere, the desolate edges of things,
leaves, stalks, the old trellis: they want to haul themselves
up onto the frame of your mind, become more than they are.

And you want to spring being from its cells,
undo the DNA, recite the world's code to itself. You want an
    explanation
for isolation, forbearance, utterance, death—
but can offer up only what troubles you. Blossoms sink into earth
and decompose. Earth, released into the air, disperses.

Elements

Water will drown you,
fire burn, air escape you,
earth bury you alive. Danger
lurks in the streets.

Witness II

Beauty on the pedestal of itself. An enigma whose
question is its own being, whose answer
is also being. The future a deal it never makes. We empty
   ourselves
of desire, lay it down as we lay down weapons.

Grief is not something to be swallowed
but a faint halo around the living, a glow. Beauty, though,
has none, walks outside at night, alone: the elocution of the stars,
unpronounceable, perfect syllables. God encrypted
in the world.

The house grows smaller at night, trying
to lose itself in thought. We listen
to the sibilance of the refrigerator keeping time. Light
through the window, the stars shedding their skins.
Beauty even in beauty, when it's easiest to forget.

Legacy: 1952

The cupboards gleamed,
the white sheets and shining silver a solitary bargain.
My grandfather a health inspector,
grandmother a genius with the iron. A match made in heaven,
aired beds and fresh pillow cases so each day
would be like the first.

Polish, the stronghold of the faithful. God may have been dead,
but it was hard to believe when He was clearly visible,
shining in every table top. The unease
that dogged His fold was bleached white, shirt collars and dresses
stiff with starch, unable to doubt without appearing ridiculous.

At least, they seemed to say, the dignity of surfaces,
devotion to a cause, preservation
of the day's radiance. Dishes and cutlery poised
and brightly, as if for a photograph, feigning assurance,
fearless.

Roses

Not because it is sufficient, but because
we subsist on light, and what doesn't
cry out to be noticed? There's something here
you might recognize, but you're not sure; still, you're willing
to risk it: the loss is of everything, seen and unseen,
the before and the after. It doesn't depend on you
but you move toward it. Because as long as there's a moment
here or there, why not arrange a few roses
in a jar, give thought to their listlessness, how they gather
the room about them yet think nothing of it, how each
thorn persists, how they have made a purpose
of holding still? Then you remember
the necessary and sufficient. This isn't it,
but you don't know where else to begin.

Argument

The fields look empty,
landing strips for light.
Primed for plurality, for excess,
we beg for *more*, hungry
for the shiver of light and dark.
It's what the world teaches:
a hundred excuses
for beauty, our minds oiled
with gorgeousness, the fields
not really empty
but so full they seem so:
wheat rustles on wheat.

Dreamlife of Houses

Darkness persists even as you waken.

Your sheets like the skin of another animal, odourless.

An ache in your limbs: you slept too little.

Close your eyes, watch your dreams disappear into the distance.
The vanishing point in your psyche.

Downstairs, the table hovers on the sill of the next day, its surface
bare as if free of thought. Things still their pale, animal selves.

Like the rim of a falls where everything waits, about to plunge.

Your heart races.

Flick the switch, and light drops from the ceiling like a bird,
stunned. Forgets to spread its wings.

Chairs sit in halos of shadow.

It's still dark. The ladder has disappeared: the night a wall you
can't climb.

Witness III

The roses, at their most adjectival,
donate themselves to charity, subside,
abstain from their own majesty.
They are the linings of themselves,
softly receive nothing,
no tribute but their own being.

The day available as a flower: take me.
Only so much time, the afternoon succoured
by its own short-lived hopes,
wanting to be everything to everyone.

A spider spins a web simply to show
there is a perfect fit between all things.
The space between the porch and the rosebush
requires no adjustment. Between the rose
and its corollaries: earth, light.

Loose and heavy, the day's drowsiness
catches up to us: sleep takes us in
like a lungful of air. Under the arch
of the porch, nothing moves.

Beholden

July, and a boy in trunks runs through
a fountain, dashing

through the transparent
beauty of the world, as we do,

goose-fleshed, shivering.
The unexplained madness: we're scared

to look up, might find ourselves
staring the gift horse in the mouth.

Water, its riches, like ropes of glass beads,
ropes of them. We don't know

the real thing though we imagine it,
living the arc of our lives under

the vault of the invisible.
But even here—a small park between

suburban houses, tame gorgeousness—beauty
can't hold still. Demands we live quickly,

brilliantly. The burden of the created.
We each know someone

who has sickened or died from it:
exhausted by its own plenitude, the world

sinks under the surface,
vanishes.

Private Lives in Public Places

Cityscape

The narrow hips of the streets.

Business an empty pedestal.

In the municipal gardens roses clamber up, intent on solitude.
Architecture, a pressure to live up to.

Watching sunsets sideways, vertical horizons at the end of day.

The city needs its failures, a measure of despair.

A childhood lisp becomes meaningless. The fear of innocence:
carry yourself as if you've always known.

Buildings, torn down, leave their silhouettes on adjoining walls
like ghosts.

The injured outlive us.

Love Poem I

The distance between things
makes me turn to you.

We have found an underground
passage through the day
where time cannot go. Where the stars
travel. In this darkness we learn
to bear witness: the ache, we are so far
from the born, the living. It will take hundreds
of years to reach the Earth. We are patient,
our pockets filled with stones.

Days in Between I

The day is a cruise ship, an ocean liner pulling into port. Leisurely train of light in its wake.

We stand at the rail, each alone.

No reason to want for other pleasures.

Our unknown selves wait on shore, staring. In the shadowed rooms of the afterlife we will meet.

Cargo: risks we won't take, names we won't part from. Fears precious as orchids.

Mid-afternoon. The cabin windows gleam.

A thud against the prow, the anchor drops: tomorrow our real lives begin.

Love Poem II

The aspen roll back the whites
of their eyes, panicked. Winds
coming in from the North.

First snow
and I still haven't
kissed you.

The neighbours' bedsheets
on the line, the privacy
of inner life everywhere now.
Bare trees, naked lawn.

Waking up to a room
where light beats its wings
like a trapped bird.

The thin hum of phone lines:
your voice is clearer in the cold.

Wickaninnish

The litter of splintered wood
at the top of the beach, the silver edge
time leaves on things. The past,
and the moment when it shines a little.
From here it seems further than ten miles
to the horizon, but they say
that's as far as you see. The sun
goes down and the logs take it to heart,
an orange glow. Illegible
rings in the wood: you are too young
to fully grasp the languages
in what you see. Concentrate,
and a glimmer of purpose may reveal itself,
but the unknown will still seek you,
laying its tinder inside you. The sun is stronger
than any of us. The logs, spread on the shore,
allow themselves to go blind.
They aren't afraid of fire.

January

Winter's cold furnace clicks
on, hums. The day pushes us slowly
toward a heavy, locked
door. No one wants to go outside.

At night, the stars, like children,
are strapped into their seats, not knowing
when they'll arrive.

Love Poem III

Vast distances in my heart
I cross all day. I go home at night
and wait for you. Loneliness now
has a shape, a purpose.
I think of train stations, domed
ceilings, pigeons, old houses. Places where time
has been emptied.

Harbour View

Ships roam the bay,
change places

like the weather, clouds.
Hour hands that move

stealthily
around flat clockfaces.

The day won't move on
without you,

is stranded, a room you enter
where clouds bloom

heavy as peonies,
petal-thick rain.

Something is begun
which can never finish:

the wall of the invisible,
the sky, is missing

several bricks.
One of them is your life.

The horizon starts
to grey. The ships,

moored to inevitability,
withhold secrets.

Poem

The poem wants to be an extra bone
in the body. Lonely,
it wants the day to come back for it:
a jacket left at the coat check,
the dance floor deserted.

There is no wisdom in the poem,
but it repeats its small life as many times
as we ask. The poem is everybody's
mother, remembering what can't be found,
remembering who you are, remembering
what hasn't even happened yet.

In the Mountains

Where emptiness comes to be alone.

An animal that has lost its lower jaw, snow-capped molars and incisors.

You climb all afternoon. When panic sets in, you've left home.

The stillness. Mountains like birds that stay all winter.

Light moults from their backs; they seem to grow younger as hours pass.

If you could be as unconcerned.

The train sends its whistle up, and up, and you pause, wait for it to hit the ceiling. The time it takes to learn patience.

The sky a broken bridge.

Implicit endlessness. Waterfalls that disappear before they hit the ground.

Dreams

At night your mind
has nothing to do but listen
to itself hum, a cloud of insects behind glass,
attracted to the glow of your sleep.

Like pulling on a pair
of long gloves—not to repair or
dissect, but to feel your heart's work
with invisible hands.

When you wake up, a slight
change inside you. Your suitcase
was searched. Everything's still there
but shifts
when you pick it up.

Love Poem IV

The sun slaps itself
on the wall like a fresh coat of paint.
Awake, we listen to each other
breathe. The fragility of time,
its uncertainties. Handed down
generation to generation, like family heirlooms:
our consciousness, our waking hours. The morning
light perjures itself, says we have more time
than we know what to do with.
You turn to me: sometimes the soul
wants to be all windows.

Calgary

The city, a glass bottle left
upright in the middle of the prairie.

Each thing an echo
inside itself.

Trees flutter like eyelids opening.

Canada geese fly through the tunnel
of glass as though it were the trough of a wave.
A parted sea of light and windows.
One chance to make it.

They duck under the moon, which still
hangs idly in the sky, passes out handbills
on which nothing is printed.
Clocks think minutes through.

The sky an old, overstuffed
armchair in which no one lounges.

Days in Between II

The long afternoon—a child wanting to be lifted and carried,
heavier than we thought.

The trauma of brightness.

The traffic is tired, can't find its destination.

It slows, wilts.

We've stopped on the shoulder, pretend we've arrived in the middle
of things and it's where we belong.

Take out the road map, have another look.

The lift in the air when a truck breezes past.

The highways have bloomed and bloomed until their splendour
wears us out.

Love Poem V

The coals of loneliness shimmer
when you come near.

The trees are being pulled slowly
back into the ground.

We haven't much to hold us.

In the sky, a few clouds, solitary
swimmers far out at sea.

Heed

Prayer I

We are like smoke
rising into the world. Thin and quick
to lose ourselves. The cathartic light
of morning catches us up,
lifts our thoughts from our minds.

Spring: winter's phantom limb
stirring. Cars like vertebrae
lead into the lobes of a primitive
intelligence, sun on the horizon.
Darkness shines like a new skin.

Loot your own heart, break the
windows, reach in and take everything
because you might not be back.
If you leave the key behind, gleaming
on its hook, it will bear witness.

Use without uses, the world becomes
the key. Your heart becomes
the world's emptiness.

Self-Reliance

The rain climbs its own shadow
to the sky: emptiness
slipped like a glove over a willing hand.
Clouds turn their backs on the public, roofs and awnings
forsaken: even the clock tower belongs to itself.

The paradox of being wanted and let go,
of wanting and letting go. Instinct stills us
as we watch the rain
disappear up the sky like the spider in the rhyme.
Whatever the world wants us to believe, we will believe,
keeping other glimpses to ourselves:
how even the stars are helpless, waiting for someone
to come and bathe them, change the sheets,
empty the bedpan. The stars, pretending they need only
to be left alone
            while silence comes, does its chores.

Canoeing the St. John River

Reeds hover on the brink
of disappearing, lilies so white they're barely
present, child-like in their proximity
to the timeless.
                    As the light confesses
to impure thoughts, a lecherous heart, we listen.
It wants a verdict, something to call its own,
but we can only hear it out:
                              at certain distances
we become helpless, image of the earth's
own helplessness. Things retreat so far
into themselves that surfaces seem evacuated.
We don't know what to make of what we see,
choices between equal uncertainties:
sky, water, lilies. Who knows if there's an inner life.

Flatrock, January 1, 2002

The ocean locks horns with itself,
rutting. Deeper, ponders
its own might.

Light grazes among the houses,
picks over garbage in the fence links.
Dogs bark at no one.
Freshly painted car park
on the wharf, no cars, no boats.

At night, the stars shine
like a cure that won't be discovered
for years.

Sympathy

I, I, I. Abandoned mine shafts
descending to voiceless
tunnels. Look up through the dark,
the world a pinprick above.

The blindness of perception, what we seek
never quite available, reflections skimmed
off the surface. In the garden, leaves twitch like sleeping
animals; a fly washes its face. You turn away, exhausted:
the abundance of the hidden.

At the bottom of the dark
shaft of the self, the impossible
waits behind a small window. Though you can bend
back the bars, you can't force
your way in. Denied access even to what
you most want: yourself, selfless.

Pacific Rim

The ocean slips
off the shore, leaves a thin
film on the sand
like a slug's trail.
Broad and silver
it lays itself out
as the tide recedes.
It tries to tell you
like a mirror: look,
see, the sky
under your feet. Elusive,
a dare, an inch
of water enough
to drown in. Everything
that happened to you
begins here. And you could fall
through it.

Bounty

Wading through the day's
luminous waste, overcome by prosperity
in which it's impossible
to care enough. Leaves thick on the ground,
every heart tunnelling
into itself.

God, it's said, picks up
the slack, but we wonder what he knows
about us. Distance,
says Weil, is His love, mark
of His own loss. But after loss,
what? How to deal
with the thickness of being?
We're crippled by hearts
we quickly outgrow—a world where need
is greater than any fear or hope.

The light, autistic, stares without speaking
at the forehead of the afternoon.
Indecision: while we tend
the wounded, the day bleeds to death
on our doorstep.

Prayer II

Insomnia: fear of the empty boat
moored in the heart. Of the space
inside the world. Of the black
lining behind mirrors.

The moon is the stump of a tree,
no growth rings. Fear of disappearance,
your own. Fear of looking over your shoulder
at no past.

The vanity that sends us
into the world to speak our names
is the one
that keeps us up at night

listening for echoes.
If you close your eyes
the world will cease. The stars don't
reassure you. Fear them also.

St. John River, Spring

As though the trees too have
predators and are ready
to flee, listening for what
they hope isn't there. Waiting
in stillness, the current barely
visible, faint tattoo
on the river's back. Floodwater.
Where swallows gather,
pale at the throats, a warning.
The clouds send down their reflections.
The difficult season.

Suffering

Here the seeds of elsewhere's destruction,
the fruits of elsewhere's labour:
invisible backhoes on ghostly soil
tripped over again and again,
debts piling up on the doorsteps of glass buildings.

At twenty-nine, already
I could spend all my time pondering what little
has happened to me. Privilege, its bought goods
massed like a sound barrier: in the distance
unheard atrocities, faint echoes
that won't penetrate for years.

War in Other Countries

The sun fixes us in place. We have no option.
Plate glass windows reflect the glare
as we peer into the safety of objects, objects, objects.
The density of being here, our lives an unearned
rescue. Leisurely, wind flips back the corners
of our jackets, reveals the lining.

Distance darkens the roofs. We listen intently,
hum of electricity: fragile means to fragile ends.
Thin threads easily broken. We keep watch
over the city, unknown monument to unknown crisis.

Shelter

A suburb near the airport. You got used
to planes passing overhead, the dull roar, the pressure
in your chest as though you were under water.
Hardly noticed the glasses rattling in the kitchen cabinet
as though they'd all had the same nightmare—
like foreign correspondents, each a report
from the fringe, trying to alert you to the possible
disaster. But you didn't believe in abroad.

When you left home you started dreaming
of planes. You sat up with your head ringing; the darkness
disoriented you, had come closer.

The enviable house in the safe hug of the cul-de-sac:
even now, you wake up from the dream
and barely hear the world around you.
Safety has stopped up your ears—it started years ago,
when the insulated walls dulled
the engines. Outside was no world
but the sprinkler-fed lawn. The glasses in the cabinet rang
like distant telephones someone else would answer.

Illusion

The light at the end of day,
shopfronts like peeling
gold, going back to the darkness
in their basements.

Bells still dangle invitingly,
but no one wants to buy.
Window displays no longer
gratify, the cash register
hardly consoling. Our urges
are like children: we will gather
them into our laps, soothe them, spend quality
time together. We've only just
realized how much they need us.

Beaten, for the moment, at the game
no one else is playing, stores slump
back to the workaday life
of goods waiting on shelves,
racks of dresses in sizes
no one wants to admit
they fit into. Cardboard boxes
in storage. They'll wait.
They've done it before.

June 15

The dandelions glow, seedlings
of light. The fields,
all arrival, laid out for something
that's just been born. Steady, steady—
first steps into afternoon.

Pretend we haven't been here
before. Pretend we don't know:
the cows gone to seed,
dandelions past their prime, shadows
in the stomach of the barn.
The emptiness of the here and now,
the end invisible, cloaked
in presence. No one asks for mercy
because where we are seems final.

Inevitable pressure of the sun. The cows
on their knees. White gloss of seeds
absorbing indecision:
                              near, nearer, nearest.

Ways of Leaving

At the Platform, Newcastle

We were playing at the edge
of the here and now where anything's
possible, so

there was none of the pain
you'd expect until the train pulled
out and the piece of us
that is time
                    ripped apart.

Now the train hobbles
along the tracks, and we're suddenly grown
back to our real sizes: what we should
have said, could have done, but

we hated goodbyes,
or so we said as the train swayed,

a clumsy
too-big man-made model of the way
everything leaves us,
                    awkwardly.

From Spadina Station

The streetcar slides into darkness, brushes past the huge
black cat that paces in your dreams. Its flank

presses against the window—how your dreamlife seeps
into waking hours and you greet the terrors of the night

with familiarity, almost affection: you are just beyond reach.
Outside, pedestrians stand under the scaffolding

of the known, wait for it to collapse while the streetcar,
your surrogate, pushes unafraid into the night, glides ahead
       on its track.

A round sign shines like a moon outside the bank: your stop:
you insert yourself into the streets' thoughts

like a ticket into a slot. They expected if not you, someone.
But there has to be more to it, and all the way home

you wonder what to do. Persistence, the habit of being here,
won't be enough. Half-asleep already, key in the lock. Raccoons, thugs

with deft hands, pry open garbage bins in the back alley.
The fluorescent lights are dim: the cat pads down the hall.

Prairie

Checking the world
like a mailbox, waiting for a message.
Watching through the screen door, a pixelated
landscape of expectation.

Summertime:
the sun has parked its car
in front of your door
and refuses to move. No one
to tow it away.

Whatever you're waiting for
won't come soon. Fields ramble on and on
about nothing in particular.

Inferences

In the laundromats clothes spin, peaceful
as falling snow. We are each quarantined by our own thoughts,
watching our feet as we walk. The day serious,
like a child learning to read;
paper in the street blows unconcerned.

Coo of pigeons: the present, its familiar sidewalks,
becomes a learned uncertainty. Awnings raised over entrances
protectively, for our own good. But we're still nervous,
keep small, overnight bags
packed in each others' hearts, ready for a quick getaway.

The Twelve Days of Christmas

Even if there had been snow, what could
it have told us? The children
are asleep, and no matter how much you want
to help out, nothing needs to be done.
The dun-coloured grass, bare
fences, empty sky. Time demands less of us
than we have to give.

So here we are, craning
our necks skyward, desiring the weight
of snow on the roof, pressed against
the house. A sign that we belong.
Partridges, pear trees, golden
rings: those things we have inherited but which
are of no account, good deeds without
any bearing on what's at hand.

God's lesson, his absence—that's
what we feel now. Religious vertigo,
dizziness that is the same
as being empty,
that is not the same as doubt
or belief.

Extinction

One by one they step
onto a barge that floats on a dark
river. Boarding in no particular order, unhurried.

They don't recognize themselves in
National Geographic pictures anymore.
Something in the eyes—a lock
on a door they can't remember having
opened. They lead a parenthetical existence
inside the world they're leaving, their past lives
a small cage in which they pace.

The boat slows down in the Amazon.
It's getting crowded. They try to relax, learn
the vernacular of eternity. But even as it
carries them over the edge

of the known world: danger
in the air, the scent of what's left on earth.
This is just the beginning.

If they could send a last message tied to the foot
of the last passenger pigeon. But it's chained
to the afterlife, gets only as far as the long-dead kings and queens
who still look greedily at the world through the wrong
end of a telescope, its beauties
tiny, receding in the convex lens.

Yet they've been disrobed; it doesn't matter now
what they decree. In eternity, they can confuse
the future with the past, make
as many mistakes as they like. They wave to CEOs
in marble-floored boardrooms. Consequences
an anchor left behind in another world.

Torbay, December 2001

After days foggy and dull-witted—a shaft
of sunlight appears and your spine,
a pawnshop appliance, is plugged in and proves
to be working. Cars shine, the fog
itself shines as things rediscover function,
purpose, the joy of travelling from a to b.
Harmless pleasures. Nature innocent
and sweet-tempered, the criminal element vanished,
just a burbling stream in the roadside gutters,
waiting for the sun to go back in,
waiting for it not to.

English Daisies

When late noon
flexes its forearm,
they ripple.

So numerous; their small advice is to admit
nothing:
        not me, not me, not me...

Precipitate
of ambition, its thoughtless
plurality:

they don't ask who you are, but how many. A selfishness all
their own, a circleless inner circle
no one breaches.

Shadow slopes over
the lawn, the slow burial
at the end of day,

the daisies the last
to go.

Age

We part from ourselves,
the doorstep dark
with fallen leaves, the wind a fire
in the branches,

the whole of creation
a fire *kindling in measures*
and in measures
going out.

Ancestors weep
through us. We turn our faces
to the sky, hard as quartz
scraped across

by planes. If Heraclitus
had a thought, it's buried
in the engines, earth
forced into air.

St. Phillip's

Wallflowers, the islands
scattered offshore,
silent. The sky
a telephone that doesn't ring.

As the day's slow illness
takes us over, we are not sad
nor are we comforted. No one really
believes in death or dying,

its unwilled oblivion. The weight, instead,
of living, its massive edifice: we'll be buried alive.

Patience

A View of Bell Island, October 2001

The wind grooms the fields, licks
their fur.

War grows tall, undisturbed
on its slender stalk.

No one walks down to the water today.

Shadowed cliffs
like stables where dark horses
wait.

Stars invisible in daylight.

Atget: *The Milkman's Horse*

Seized and shaken by an invisible
hand, her head a frenzy, swarm of light.
As though her very being
were a bridle she tries to shake off.

Isolated on the page as though in quarantine,
she is institutionalized behind the walls of the imaginable.
We want to touch her the way we want to touch the edge of a
    deep
wound. To feel light slippery on our wrists. The brightest mirror
in which everything we dread might happen.

The long exposure.
A row of dark windows behind her.
A street that could be our own.

Dusk

The moment you've been waiting for, when a thing turns
into its opposite, a reason for compassion. The tinnitus of traffic
    in the city,
funnelled into darkness. Every lit object an injury. Every change
    a wish.

In the garden, shrubs and plants go blind. Trees stare away
from them like patients in a waiting room, thoughts folded in their
    laps. Everything is leaving
by holding still. The dusk deepens flowers. The silence is an
    operating room.

Our passions thin, liquify. The house behind us has darkened
until it isn't recognizable. Fails. Under the surgical gaze of the stars
we bare ourselves, wait to see what can be done.

Second View of Bell Island, October 2001

A thinking stillness.

Patience, its small, useless
vessels. The ferryboat
rocked by the ocean's
deep pendulum.

Perplexed by silence,
war opens its parachute, slips
into the ocean,
settles.

We travel quietly, so as not
to draw attention to ourselves. The waves
slip like thread
in and out of the eye of a needle.

First Snow

The pain of visibility, the trees
unbribable, backs against the sky.
No exchange. Not a way of dreaming but a persistent
wakefulness, pinching the nerves
when the heart wants to feel nothing.
Snow can be a man who still thinks of himself as a child,
invisible. But nothing is more obvious than his hunched
     shoulders.

Birds sink into their plumage,
shake the cold from their backs. There is too much light
and it's too strong: all you want to do is remember,
but the day insists on a witness. What's past is less than this.
Its opposite, a drift of white, settles over the lawn.

Night Fare

Taxis float like water lilies
on the slick tarmac. It's raining
too hard to walk, and it's late, they argue.
They want to take you home.

The rise and fall of your heartbeat,
cabs pulling in and out from the curb, hoping
you'll climb in. But they know too much about you,
the shine of each door a warning.
You won't give them the satisfaction.

As you walk home, the stages of sleep
uncurl like a fist in upper stories of houses.
The night shuffles its deck of cards, plays games
with your subconscious:
                              after you've undressed,
when you're looking out your window,
you'll see your mind galloping by. Later,
you close your eyes: the flash of mane as it turns
the corner, just before
you start to dream.

Forever

Too young to be convinced, you can't imagine
that time might turn itself inside out, showing
that what you thought was the infinite
was only its lining. Slippery and easily frayed,
your whole life a kind of magic trick.

You rehearse your own funeral, who will attend,
who will be sorry, how death will somehow prove you right.
Submerged in thoughts of this death like a bath,
right up to the neck, still breathing.

What you don't want to imagine is how far it will take you
from the known: your friends and relatives will watch your life
close into a fist, from which, when you take your last breath,
they will pull a square of bright silk. They'll slide it through their
    fingers
then let it go, watch it drift away. And when they're ready,
they'll open the fist to show it's empty.

Third View of Bell Island, December 2001

The sky's density sunken
into the soil. The invisible
come home to roost. Fields lay back
their ears, expecting a wind
that hasn't arrived.

Civilization has rubbed itself raw
on the cliffs and resents its wounds.
The ocean: train upon train arrives,
unmet, on the shore.

Because It Comes Late, If at All

December dark runs its hands
through late afternoon.

The single
injury of birth from which we
never recover, yearning to restore ourselves
to wisdom:
>   *please, please—*
like pigeons pleading in the streets,
though our own voices are harder to hear.

We perjure ourselves
when we step out the door, ignoring
the intrusive facts of death and time. We open
the afternoon like a newspaper, as though
it has nothing to do with us. Patients

in a waiting room, we stare at the clock
without thinking what it means—
but we bear witness. The news is of a desert
we're crossing, the shadow that comes
earlier these days.

Nocturne

Night sky a clear-cut, stumped
with tiny stars. Sage, furred, soft and silver
in the garden. The house grows large
with silence. Sleepless. Behind every door,
a ruined city.

Time is urban sprawl: the hours go on forever.
You wait out your thoughts. Patience, virtue of solitude.

False dawn. When you sleep at last,
you become an abandoned house on a hill.
Outside, the mountains, like huge gravestones,
lie low under the stars.

Untitled

Sleep: a long, dim-lit tunnel
through winter. Dusk presses
at your back. Everything
you could have dreamed

is leaving, a line of geese
overhead. This is memory
slipping away. This is thought before
you were born.

As if sitting under the slope
of a dark hill. Time to put away
childish things. No honking,
the geese like a car late
at night, disappearing.

When they've gone,
the light will go deeper
into itself. Thought will hibernate.

This is the last dream you will have
before winter.

Thanks:

to Jan Zwicky for bringing the full weight of her attention and concern to bear in editing these poems,

also to Don McKay for general, ongoing support and encouragement

to Sophie Thériault for the cover art and so much more

to Wyll River

to Ross Leckie, Anne Simpson, Eric Hill, Ken Howe, Adam Dickinson, Shane Rhodes, Michael deBeyer, Evan Jones, Darren Lee, George Sipos and Mark Truscott

to the Victoria College workshop

to Kitty Lewis for her cheerful organizational skill and Maureen Harris for her clear-headed and appreciative approach to the poems

to the Canada Council for the Arts, the Ontario Arts Council and the Toronto Arts Council, without which I wouldn't be able to do what I do

to the Banff Centre, where some of these poems were born

to the people and institutions who have invited me to read

and to my family, including our Columbian and Chinese additions.

Versions of these poems have appeared in *Arc*, *The Fiddlehead*, *Grain*, *The Literary Review of Canada*, and *The Malahat Review*. Thanks also to these publications for their support.

Sue Sinclair has published poetry and reviews in journals across Canada. Her first book of poems, *Secrets of Weather & Hope* (Brick Books, 2001) was shortlisted for the 2002 Gerald Lampert Award. Sue grew up in Newfoundland and currently lives in Toronto.

How Do You Feel?

Cynthia MacGregor

Rosen Classroom Books and Materials
New York

Published in 2002 by The Rosen Publishing Group, Inc.
29 East 21st Street, New York, NY 10010

Copyright © 2002 by The Rosen Publishing Group, Inc.

All rights reserved. No part of this book may be reproduced in any form without permission in writing from the publisher, except by a reviewer.

Book Design: Ron A. Churley

Photo Credits: Cover, p. 1 © Jim Whitmer/FPG International; p. 4 © FPG International; pp. 5, 14 © VCG/FPG International; pp. 6, 7, 15 © SuperStock; p. 9 © Corbis; p. 10 © Ron Chapple/FPG International; pp. 11, 17 © Arthur Tilley/FPG International; p. 13 © J. Marshall/The Image Works; p. 19 © Scott Barrow/International Stock; p. 21 © Jeff Greenberg/International Stock.

ISBN: 0-8239-8230-0
6-pack ISBN: 0-8239-8633-0

Manufactured in the United States of America

Contents

"How Do You Feel?"

Sometimes people ask you how you feel. Usually they want to know if you feel

well. Feeling well and feeling sick aren't the only kinds of feelings we have. We also have feelings inside of us.

We can have happy emotions every day.

We can feel happy, sad, angry, **jealous** (JEL-us), lonely, or afraid. These feelings are called **emotions**. Emotions are very powerful. They make a difference in how you feel and act every day. Your emotions can be happy or unhappy.

We can have unhappy emotions every day.

5

Your Choice

Your emotions can change the way you feel and act toward other people. Your **actions** may get good or bad **reactions** from other people. We always have a

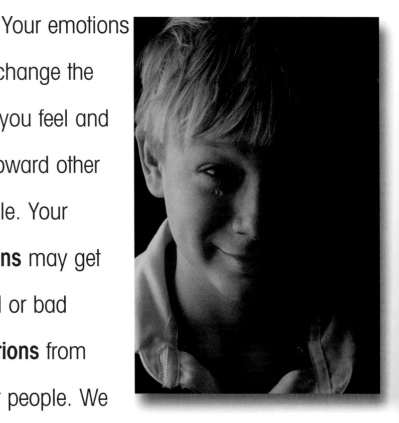

Crying is one way to deal with a sad feeling.

choice about how we want to handle feeling angry, sad, or jealous.

Yelling at someone when you are mad will get a different reaction than trying to tell that person how you feel in a calm way.

Everyone has control over how they handle their feelings.

7

Mind and Body

Your feelings can change the way you act. Your feelings can even change the way your body looks and feels. When you are happy, you may smile and feel good inside. When you feel sad or angry, you may feel sick inside. When you are afraid of something, you may get a stomachache. Since your mind and body work together, when an emotion makes you feel bad, your body may not feel well either. Some people believe that when we aren't happy, it's easier for our bodies to get sick.

Taking care of your body and your mind will help you stay healthy.

9

Happiness

When you feel happy, you feel good inside. You can show you are happy by being friendly to others. You can be happy

Sometimes happiness is a quiet, content feeling inside of you.

doing something by yourself, such as playing a game on the computer. You can choose to think **positive** thoughts and be happy whenever you want to.

Doing things you enjoy with friends and family can make you feel happy. Playing a game of soccer or going to a movie together are just a few ways to share happy times with others.

We feel happy when we do things that we enjoy.

Jealousy

Everyone feels jealous from time to time. There may be times when a friend gets to buy something you wanted for yourself. Sometimes you may feel jealous of another person when you think he or she is getting more attention than you are. When you feel jealousy toward another person, you don't feel good inside.

Feeling jealous of someone may make you feel like you want to cry. You may want to say something mean to make that person feel bad. You should think about how your actions may make another person feel.

Sharing your feelings with an adult you trust
can help you deal with different emotions.

Sadness

Sometimes you might feel sad. It could be that someone hurt your feelings or a close friend moved away. Sometimes things we can't control make us feel sad. Doing things you enjoy will help you deal with some of the sad feelings.

Everyone goes through times when something makes them feel sad.

Talking to a friend about your feelings may help. Writing a letter to your friend who moved away will help you feel closer to

him or her. Writing your thoughts in a **journal** can help you understand why you are sad.

Talking to a parent or other adult about why you are sad can help you feel better.

Anger

You may feel angry when someone does something you don't like. Everyone has different ways of dealing with anger. Some people choose to keep their feelings inside. This may not help them deal with the problem. Others may yell at the person they are angry with. This usually gets both people more **upset**. Finding a place where you can let your anger out will help you feel better. Go into your bedroom and punch a pillow or write about your feelings in your journal. Talk to someone about why you feel this way.

Talking to the person you were angry with after you have calmed down may help the two of you understand each other's feelings. Understanding why you were angry may help you find an answer to the problem.

It helps to be able to talk to someone about feeling angry and the best ways to handle it.

Fear

Feeling afraid of something or someone can make you uneasy. Hearing a strange noise or being alone in the dark can make you afraid. Doing something you have never done before can make you feel nervous.

Sometimes facing up to what scares you can help you get past your fear. Sometimes talking to your parents or an adult you trust about your fears can help you feel better. Then you can **solve** the problem and deal with what is scaring you.

Sometimes it helps to tell someone when you feel afraid.

Getting Over It

Part of getting over emotions that make you feel bad is trying to understand why you feel the way you do. If you get a bad grade on a test, it's okay to feel sad. You can think of ways to do better on the next test.

If something happens to make you feel sad, afraid, angry, or jealous, try to figure out why you feel this way. Think of positive ways to handle your feelings and those of the people around you. Maybe you need to accept that you cannot change some things. Maybe you need to say you're sorry to someone for hurting his or her feelings.

Maybe you need to talk to someone who understands how you feel. Drawing a picture or writing about something that makes you feel unhappy can also help you deal with different emotions.

We all have to deal with unhappy emotions sometimes.

Do Something Nice for Yourself

Whether or not you can change something that has made you unhappy, you can do something to make yourself feel better. Hold your cat and listen to her purr. Read your favorite book. Spend some time with a friend, or call a friend on the phone. Play your favorite game. Listen to some music you like.

You can talk to your parents or an adult you trust about something that is bothering you. The first step is trying to understand what your emotions are when you feel them. How do you feel today?

Glossary

action   Something you do.

emotion   A feeling you have, like happiness, sadness, or anger.

jealous   Wishing you had what someone else has and feeling bad about it.

journal   A daily written record of what a person does, thinks, and feels.

positive   Good or helpful.

reaction   An action or reply that is caused by another action.

solve   To find the answer to something.

upset   Very unhappy.

Index